I0445708

FRIENDSHIP

BY

MARCUS TULLIUS CICERO

FRANCIS BACON

RALPH WALDO EMERSON

WITH PORTRAITS

Fredonia Books
Amsterdam, The Netherlands

Friendship

by
Marcus Tullius Cicero
Francis Bacon
Ralph Waldo Emerson

ISBN: 1-58963-985-5

Copyright © 2002 by Fredonia Books

Reprinted from the 1891 edition

Fredonia Books
Amsterdam, The Netherlands
http://www.fredoniabooks.com

All rights reserved, including the right to reproduce
this book, or portions thereof, in any form.

In order to make original editions of historical works
available to scholars at an economical price, this
facsimile of the original edition of 1891 is
reproduced from the best available copy and has
been digitally enhanced to improve legibility, but the
text remains unaltered to retain historical
authenticity.

DE AMICITIA

(CONCERNING FRIENDSHIP)

BY

MARCUS TULLIUS CICERO

TRANSLATED BY

CYRUS R. EDMONDS

"A friend cannot be known in prosperity, and an enemy cannot be hid in adversity. True friends visit us in prosperity only when invited, but in adversity they come without invitation."—*Theophrastus*.

"The friends thou hast and their adoption tried,

Grapple them to thy soul with hooks of steel."—*Shakespeare*.

"When two friends part they should lock up each others' secrets and exchange keys."

DE AMICITIA.

QUINTUS MUCIUS, the augur, used to relate many
things of Caius Lælius, his father-in-law, from memory
and in a pleasant manner, and did not scruple in every
discourse to call him a wise man. Moreover, I myself,
after assuming the manly toga, was introduced by my
father to Scævola, in such a way that, as far as I could
and it was permitted me, I never quitted the old man's
side. Accordingly, many sagacious discussions of his,
and many short and apt sayings, I committed to memory, and desired to become better informed by his wisdom. When he died I betook myself to Scævola, the
pontiff, who is the only man in our country that I ven-
ture to pronounce the most distinguished for talent and
for integrity. But of him elsewhere. I now return to
the augur. Among many other circumstances, I remember that once being seated at home in his arm-
chair (as was his custom), when I was in his company,
and a very few of his intimate friends, he fell by
chance upon that subject of discourse which at the time
was in the mouth of nearly every one; for you of course
remember Atticus, and the more so because you were
very intimate with Publius Sulpicius (when he, as trib-

une of the people, was estranged by a deadly hatred
from Quintus Pompey, who was then consul, with
whom up to that time he had lived on terms of the
closest union and affection), how great was the surprise
and even regret of the people. Accordingly, when
Scævola had incidentally mentioned that very subject,
he laid before us the discourse of Lælius on Friendship,
which had been addressed by the latter to himself and
to the other son-in-law of Lælius, Caius Fannius, the
son of Marcus, a few days after the death of Africanus.
The opinions of that disquisition I committed to memory, and in this book I have set them forth according
to my own judgment. For I have introduced the individuals as if actually speaking, lest " said I " and " said
he " should be too frequently interposed; and that the
dialogue might seem to be held by persons face to face.
For when you were frequently urging me to write something on the subject of friendship, it seemed to me a
matter worthy as well of the consideration of all as of
our intimacy. I have therefore willingly done so, that
I might confer a benefit on many in consequence of
your request. But as in the Cato Major, which was
addressed to you on the subject of old age, I have introduced Cato when an old man conversing, because
there seemed no person better adapted to speak of that
period of life than he, who had been an old man for so
long a time, and in that old age had been pre-eminently

prosperous; so when I heard from our ancestors that the attachment of Caius Lælius and Publius Scipio was especially worthy of record, the character of Lælius seemed to me a suitable one to deliver these very observations on friendship which Scævola remembered to have been spoken by him. Now this description of discourses, resting on the authority of men of old, and of those of high rank, seems, I know not on what principle, to carry with it the greater weight. Accordingly, while I am reading my own writing, I am sometimes so much affected as to suppose that it is Cato, and not myself that is speaking. But as then I, an old man, wrote to you, who are an old man, on the subject of old age, so in this book I myself, a most sincere friend, have written to a friend on the subject of friendship. On that occasion Cato was the speaker, than whom there was no one at that time older or wiser. On this, Lælius, not only a wise man (for so he has been considdered), and one pre-eminent in reputation for friendship, speaks on that subject. I would wish you to withdraw your thoughts a little while from me, and fancy that Lælius himself is speaking. Caius Fannius and Quintus Mucius come to their father-in-law after the death of Africanus. With these the discourse begins. Lælius replies; and the whole of his dissertation regards friendship, which in reading you will discover for yourself.

FANNIUS. Such is the case, dear Lælius, nor was
there ever a better or more distinguished man than
Africanus. But you ought to consider that the eyes of
all are now turned upon you, Lælius; you alone they
both denominate and believe to be wise. This character was lately bestowed on M. Cato; we know that
Lucius Atilius, among our fathers, was entitled a wise
man; but each on a different and peculiar account;
Atilius, because he was considered versed in the civil
law; Cato, because he had experience in a variety of
subjects; both in the senate and in the forum many instances are recorded either of his shrewd forethought
or persevering action, or pointed reply; wherefore he
already had, as it were, the surname of wise in his old
age. While of you it is remarked that you are wise
in a different sense, not only by nature and character, but further, by application and learning; and not
as the vulgar, but as the learned designate a wise
man, such as was none in all Greece. For as those
who are called the seven wise men, persons who
inquire into such things with great nicety, do not
consider them in the class of wise men. We learn
that at Athens there was one peculiarly so, and that
he was even pronounced by the oracle of Apollo
the wisest of men. This is the kind of wisdom
they conceive to be in you, that you consider every
thing connected with you to rest upon yourself, and

consider the events of life as subordinate to virtue; therefore, they inquire of me (I believe of you also, Scævola), in what manner you bear the death of Africanus. And the rather so, because on the last nones, when we had come into the gardens of Decius Brutus, the augur, for the purpose of discussion, as our practice is, you were not present; although you were accustomed most punctually to observe that day and that engagement.

SCÆVOLA. It is true, many are inquiring, Caius Lælius, as has been asserted by Fannius. But for my part, I answer them according to what I have remarked, that you bear with patience the grief which you have suffered by the death of one who was at once a very distinguished man and a very dear friend; yet that you could not forbear being distressed, nor would that have been consistent with your feelings as a man. And with regard to your not having attended last nones at our assembly, ill-health was the cause, and not affliction.

LÆLIUS. You certainly said what was right, Scævola, and agreeable to truth; for neither ought I to have absented myself through any inconvenience of mine from that duty which I have always fulfilled when I was well, nor by any chance do I conceive it can happen to a man of firmness of character that any interruption should take place in his duty. And as for you, Fannius, who say there is attributed to me so much merit, as I am neither conscious of nor lay claim to, you act therein like a friend; but, as it seems to me, you do not form a right estimate of Cato, for either there never has been a wise man, which I rather think, or if there ever was one, he was the man. For (to omit other cases) consider how he endured the loss of his son. I remember the instance of Paullus, and witnessed that of Gallus; but theirs was in the case of children; but Cato's is that of a mature and respected man. Wherefore pause before you prefer to Cato, even him whom Apollo, as you say, pronounced the wisest of men: for the deeds of the one are praised, but only the sayings of the other. Concerning myself, however (for I would now address you both), entertain the following sentiments:

Should I say that I am not distressed by the loss of Scipio, philosophers may determine with what propriety I should do so; but assuredly I should be guilty of falsehood. For I am distressed at being bereaved of such a friend, as no one, I consider, will ever be to me again, and, as I can confidently assert, no one ever was; but I am not destitute of a remedy. I comfort myself, and especially with this consolation, that I am free from that error by which most men, on the decease of friends, are wont to be tormented; for I feel that no evil has happened to Scipio; it has befallen myself, if indeed it has happened to any. Now to be above measure distressed

at one's own troubles, is characteristic of the man who
loves not his friend, but himself. In truth, as far as he
is concerned, who can deny that his end was glorious ?
for unless he had chosen to wish for immortality, of
which he had not the slightest thought, what did he fail
to obtain which it was lawful for a man to wish for ?
A man who, as soon as he grew up, by his transcendent
merit far surpassed those sanguine hopes of his country-
men which they had conceived regarding him when a
mere boy, who never stood for the consulship, yet was
made consul twice; on the first occasion before his time;
on the second, at the proper age as regarded himself,
though for the commonwealth almost too late; who, by
overthrowing two cities, most hostile to our empire, put
an end, not only to all present, but all future wars.
What shall I say of his most engaging manners; of his
dutiful conduct to his mother; his generosity to his
sisters; his kindness to his friends; his uprightness toward
all ? These are known to you: and how dear he was to
the state, was displayed by its mourning at his death.
How, therefore, could the accession of a few years have
benefited such a man ? For although old age is not
burdensome (as I recollect Cato asserted, in conversation with myself and Scipio the year before he died),
yet it takes away that freshness which Scipio even yet
possessed. Wherefore his life was such that nothing
could be added to it, either in respect of good fortune

or of glory: moreover, the very suddenness of his death took away the consciousness of it. On which kind of death it is difficult to pronounce: what men conjecture, you yourselves know. However, this we may assert with truth, that of the many most glorious and joyous days which P. Scipio witnessed in the course of his life, that day was the most glorious when, on the breaking up of the senate, he was escorted home in the evening by the conscript fathers, by the allies of the Roman people, and the Latins, the day before he died; so that from so high a position of dignity he may seem to have passed to the gods above rather than to those below. Nor do I agree with those who have lately begun to assert this opinion, that the soul also dies simultaneously with the body, and that all things are annihilated by death.

The authority of the ancients has more weight with me, either that of our own ancestors, who paid such sacred honors to the dead which surely they would not have done if they thought these honors did in no way affect them; or that of those who once lived in this country, and enlightened, by their institutions and instructions, Magna Græcia (which now indeed is entirely destroyed, but then was flourishing); or of him who was pronounced by the oracle of Apollo to be the wisest of men, who did not say first one thing and then another, as is generally done, but always the same; namely, that the souls of men are divine, and that when they have departed from the body, a return to heaven is opened to them, and the speediest to the most virtuous and just. Which same opinion was also held by Scipio; for he indeed, a very few days before his death, as if he had a presentiment of it, when Philus and Manilius were present, and many others, and you also, Scævola, had gone with me, for three days descanted on the subject of government; of which discussion the last was almost entirely on the immortality of souls, which he said he had learned in sleep through a vision from Africanus. If this be the fact, that the spirit of the best man most easily flies away in death, as from the prison-house and chains of the body; whose passage to the gods can we conceive to have been readier than that of Scipio? Wherefore, to be afflicted at this his departure, I fear, would be the part rather of an envious person than of a friend. But if, on the other hand this be rather the truth, that the death of the soul and of the body is one and the same, and that no consciousness remains; as there is no advantage in death, so certainly there is no evil. For when consciousness is lost, it becomes the same as if he had never been born at all; yet, both we ourselves are glad, and this state as long as it shall exist, will rejoice that he was born. Wherefore (as I said above) with him indeed all ended well; with myself less happily; for it had been more equitable that, as I entered upon life first, I should likewise first depart from it. But yet I so enjoy the recollection of our friendship, that I seem to have lived happily because I lived with Scipio; with whom I had a common anxiety on public and private affairs, and with whom my life both at home and abroad was associated, and there existed that, wherein consists the entire strength of friendship, an entire agreement of inclinations, pursuits and sentiments. That character for wisdom, therefore, which Fannius a little while ago mentioned, does not so delight me, especially since it is undeserved, as the hope that the recollection of our friendship will last forever. And it is the more gratifying to me, because scarcely in the history of the world are three or four pairs of friends mentioned by name; and I indulge in the hope that the friendship of Scipio and Lælius will be known to posterity in this class.

FANNIUS. Indeed, Lælius, that must be so. But since you have made mention of friendship, and as we have leisure, you will do what is very agreeable to me (I hope also to Scævola), if, as your custom is concerning other matters when your opinion of them is asked, so you would descant on friendship, [telling us] what is your opinion, of what nature you consider it to be, and what direction you would lay down.

SCÆVOLA. To me it will be exceedingly agreeable; and in fact, when I was endeavoring to prevail with you, Fannius anticipated me; wherefore, you will confer a very great favor on both of us.

LÆLIUS. I indeed should not object, if I could feel confidence in myself; for not only is the subject a splendid one, but we, as Fannius said, have nothing to do. But who am I? or what ability is there in me for this? This is the practice of scholars, and of Grecian scholars, that a subject be given them on which they are to dispute, however suddenly. It is a great undertaking, and requires no little practice. Wherefore, as to what may be said on the subject of friendship, I recommend you to seek it from those who profess such things. I can only urge you to prefer friendship to all human possessions; for there is nothing so suited to our nature, so well adapted to prosperity or adversity. But first of all, I am of opinion, that except among the virtuous, friendship can not exist; I do not analyze this principle too closely, as they do who inquire with too great nicety into those things, perhaps, with truth on their side, but with little general advantage; for they maintain that there is no good man but the wise man. Be it so; yet they define wisdom to be such as no mortal has ever attained to; whereas, we ought to contemplate those things which exist in practice and in common life, and not the subjects of fictions or of our own wishes. I would never pretend to say that Caius Fabricius, Marius Curius, and Titus Coruncanius, whom our ancestors esteemed wise, were wise according to the standard of these moralists. Wherefore let them keep to

themselves the name of wisdom, both invidious and un-
intelligible; and let them allow that these were good
men—nay, they will not even do that; they will declare
that this can not be granted except to a wise man. Let
us therefore proceed with all our dull genius, as they
say. Those who so conduct themselves, and so live that
their honor, their integrity, their justice, and liberality
are approved; so that there is not in them any covetousness, or licentiousness, or boldness; and that they are of
great consistency, as those men whom I have mentioned
above;—let us consider these worthy of the appellation
of good men, as they have been accounted such, because
they follow (as far as men are able) nature, which is the
best guide of a good life.   For I seem to myself to have
this view, that we are so formed by nature, that there
should be a certain social tie among all; stronger, however,
as each approaches nearer to us. Accordingly, citizens
are preferable to foreigners, and relations to strangers;
for with the latter, nature herself has created a friendly
feeling, though this has not sufficient strength. For in
this respect friendship is superior to relationship, because from relationship benevolence can be withdrawn,
and from friendship it can not; for with the withdrawal
of benevolence the very name of friendship is done
away, while that of relationship remains. Now how
great the power of friendship is, may be best gathered
from this consideration, that out of the boundless society

of the human race, which nature herself has joined together, friendship is a matter so contracted, and brought into so narrow a compass, that the whole of affection is confined to two, or at any rate to very few.

Now friendship is nothing else than a complete union of feeling on all subjects, divine and human, accompanied by kindly feeling and attachment; than which, indeed, I am not aware whether, with the exception of wisdom, any thing better has been bestowed on man by the immortal gods. Some men prefer riches, others good health, others influence; others again honors, many prefer even pleasures; the last, indeed, is the characteristic of beasts; while the former are fleeting and uncertain, depending not so much on our own purpose as on the fickleness of fortune. Whereas those who place the supreme good in virtue, therein do admirably; but this very virtue itself both begets and constitutes friendship; nor without this virtue can friendship exist at all. Now let us define this virtue according to the usage of life, and of our common language, and let us not measure it, as certain learned persons do, by pomp of language; and let us include among the good those who are so accounted—the Paulli, the Catos, the Galli, the Scipios, and the Phili; with these men ordinary life is content; and let us pass over those who are nowhere found to exist. Among men of this kind, therefore, friendship finds facilities so great that I can scarcely describe them. In the first place—to whom can life be "worth living," as Ennius says, who does not repose on the mutual kind feeling of some friend? What can be more delightful than to have one to whom you can speak on all subjects just as to yourself? Where would be the great enjoyment in prosperity if you had not one to rejoice in it equally with yourself? And adversity would indeed be difficult to endure without some one who would bear it even with greater regret than yourself. In short, all other objects that are sought after are severally suited to some one single purpose; riches, that you may spend them; power, that you may be courted; honors, that you may be extolled; pleasures, that you may enjoy them; good health, that you may be exempt from harm, and perform the functions of the body. Whereas friendship comprises the greatest number of objects possible; wherever you turn yourself, it is at hand; shut out of no place, never out of season, never irksome; and therefore we do not use fire and water, as they say, on more occasions than we do friendship. And I am not now speaking of common-place or ordinary friendship (though even that brings delight and benefit), but of real and true friendship, such as belonged to those of whom very few are recorded; for prosperity friendship renders more brilliant, and adversity more supportable, by dividing and communicating it.

And while friendship embraces very many and great advantages, she undoubtedly surpasses all in this, that she shines with a brilliant hope over the future, and never suffers the spirit to be weakened or to sink. Besides, he who looks on a true friend looks, as it were, upon a kind of image of himself; wherefore friends, though absent, are still present; though in poverty, they are rich; though weak, yet in the enjoyment of health; and, what is still more difficult to assert, though dead, they are alive; so entirely does the honor, the memory, the regret of friends attend them; from which circumstance the death of the one seems to be happy, and the life of the other praiseworthy; nay, should you remove from nature the cement of kind feelings, neither a house nor a city will be able to stand; even the cultivation of the land will not continue. If it be not clearly perceived how great is the power of friendship and concord, it can be distinctly inferred from quarrels and dissensions; for what house is there so established, or what state so firmly settled, that may not utterly be overthrown by hatred and dissension? From which it may be determined how much advantage there is in friendship. They relate, indeed, that a certain learned man of Agrigentum promulgated in Greek verses the doctrine that all things which cohere throughout the whole world, and all things that are the subjects of motion, are brought together by friendship, and are dis-

pelled by discord; and this principle all men understand and illustrate by their conduct. Therefore, if at
any time any act of a friend has been exhibited, either
in undergoing or in sharing dangers, who is there that
does not extol such an act with the highest praise?
What shouts of applause were lately heard through the
whole theater on the occasion of a new play by my
guest and friend, Marcus Pacuvius, when the king, being ignorant which of them was Orestes, Pylades said
he was Orestes, that he might be put to death instead
of him; but Orestes, as was the fact, solemnly maintained that he was the man? They stood up and ap-
plauded in an imaginary case; what must we suppose
they would have done in a real one? Nature herself
excellently asserted her rightful power when men pronounced that to be rightly done in another, which they
could not do themselves. Thus far I seem to have been
able to lay down what are my sentiments concerning
friendship. If anything remains (and I fancy there is
much), ask of those, if you please, who practice such
discussions.

FANNIUS. But we would rather hear it from you,
although I have often asked such questions, and heard
their opinions, and that not without satisfaction, yet
what we desire is the somewhat different thread of your
discourse.

SCÆVOLA. You would say so still more, Fannius, if

you had been present lately in the gardens of Scipio,
when the subject of Government was discussed. What
an able pleader was he then on the side of justice
against the subtle argument of Philus!

FANNIUS. Nay, it was an easy task for the most just
of men to uphold the cause of justice.

SCÆVOLA. What shall we say then of friendship?
Would it not be easy for him to eulogize it, who, for
maintaining it with the utmost fidelity, steadiness, and
integrity, has gained the highest glory?

LÆLIUS. Why, this is using force against one: for
what matters it by what kind of request you compel me?
You, certainly do compel me. For to oppose the wishes
of one's sons-in-law, especially in a good matter, is not
only hard, but it is not even just. After very often,
then, reflecting on the subject of friendship, this question seems to me especially worthy of consideration,
whether friendship has become an object of desire, on
account of weakness or want, so that by giving and re-
ceiving favors, each may receive from another, and
mutually repay, what he is himself incapable of acquir-
ing. Or whether this is only a property of friendship;
while there is another cause, higher and nobler and more
directly derived from nature herself. For love (from
which friendship takes its name) is the main motive for
the union of kind feelings: for advantages truly are
often derived from those who are courted under a pre-

tense of friendship, and have attention paid them for a temporary purpose. In friendship there is nothing false, and nothing pretended; and whatever belongs to it is sincere and spontaneous. Wherefore friendship seems to me to have sprung rather from nature than from a sense of want, and more from an attachment of the mind with a certain feeling of affection, than from a calculation how much advantage it would afford. And of what nature indeed it is, may be observed in the case of certain beasts; for they love their offspring up to a certain time, and are loved by them in such a way that their emotions are easily discovered. And this is much more evident in man. In the first place, from that affection which subsists between children and parents, which can not be destroyed without detestable wickedness: next, where a similar feeling of love has existed, if we have met with any one with whose character and disposition we sympathize, because we appear to discover in him a certain effulgence as it were of integrity and virtue. For nothing is more amiable than virtue, nothing which more strongly allures us to love it, seeing that because of their virtue and integrity we can in a certain degree love those whom we have never seen. Who can mention the name of Caius Fabricius, and Marius Curius, otherwise than with love and affection, though he never saw them? Who can forbear hating Tarquinius Superbus, Spurius Cassius, and Spurius Mælius? Against two generals we had a struggle for empire in Italy, I mean Pyrrhus and Hannibal; toward the former, on account of his honorable conduct, we bear not a very hostile disposition; while this state will always detest the latter for his cruelty.

Now if such be the influence of integrity, that we love it even in those whom we have never seen, and, what is much more, even in an enemy, what wonder if men's feelings are affected when they seem to discover the goodness and virtue of those with whom they may become connected by intercourse? although love is confirmed by the reception of kindness, and by the discovery of an earnest sympathy, and by close familiarity; which things being added to the first emotion of the mind and the affections, there is kindled a large amount of kindly feeling. And if any imagine that this proceeds from a sense of weakness, so that there shall be secured a friend, by whom a man may obtain that which he wants, they leave to friendship a mean indeed, and, if I may so speak, any thing but respectable origin, when they make her to be born of indigence and want; were this the case, then in proportion as a man judged that there were the least resources in himself, precisely in that degree would he be best qualified for friendship; whereas the fact is far otherwise. For just as a man has most confidence in himself, and as he is most completely fortified by worth and wisdom, so that he needs

no one's assistance, and feels that all his resources reside
in himself; in the same proportion he is most highly distinguished for seeking out and forming friendships.
For what did Africanus want of me? nothing whatever;
nor indeed did I need aught from him: but I loved him
from admiration of his excellence; he in turn perhaps
was attached to me from some high opinion which he
entertained of my character, and association fostered our
affection. But although many and great advantages en-
sued, yet it was not from any hope of these that the
cause of our attachment sprang; for as we are beneficent
and liberal, not to exact favor in return (for we are not
usurers in kind actions), but by nature are inclined to
liberality, thus I think that friendship is to be desired,
not attracted by the hope of reward, but because the
whole of its profit consists in love only. From such
opinions, they who, after the fashion of beasts, refer
everything to pleasure, widely differ: and no great
wonder, since they cannot look up to any thing lofty,
magnificent, or divine, who cast all their thoughts on an
object so mean and contemptible. Therefore let us exclude such persons altogether from our discourse; and
let us ourselves hold this opinion, that the sentiment of
loving, and the attachment of kind feelings, are produced
by nature, when the evidence of virtue has been established; and they who have eagerly sought the latter, draw
nigh and attach themselves to it, that they may enjoy

the friendship and character of the individual they have begun to love, and that they may be commensurate and equal in affection, and more inclined to confer a favor than to claim any return. And let this honorable struggle be maintained between them: so not only will the greatest advantages be derived from friendship, but its origin from nature rather than from a sense of weakness, will be at once more impressive and more true. For if it were expediency that cemented friendships, the same when changed would dissolve them; but because nature can never change, therefore true friendships are eternal. Thus you see the origin of friendship, unless you wish to make some reply to these views.

FANNIUS. Nay, go on, Lælius, for I answer for Scævola here (who is my junior) on my own authority.

SCÆVOLA. You do right; wherefore let us attend.

LÆLIUS. Listen, then, my excellent friends, to the discussion which was very frequently held by me and Scipio on the subject of friendship; although he indeed used to say that nothing was more difficult than that friendship should continue to the end of life; for it often happened, either that the same course was not expedient to both parties, or that they held different views of politics: he also remarked that the characters of men often changed; in some cases by adversity, in others by old age becoming oppressive; and he derived an authority for such notions from a comparison with early life, because the strongest attachments of boys are constantly laid aside with the prætexta; even if they should maintain it to manhood, yet sometimes it is broken off by rivalry, for a dowried wife, or some other advantage, which they cannot both attain. And even if men should be carried on still further in their friendship, yet that feeling is often undermined, should they fall into rivalry for preferments; for there is no greater enemy to friendship than covetousness of money, in most men, and even in the best, an emulous desire of high offices and glory; in consequence of which the most bitter enmities have often arisen between the dearest friends. For great dissensions, and those in most instances, justifiable, arise, when some request is made of friends which is improper; as, for instance, that they should become either the ministers of their lust or their supporters in the perpetration of wrong; and they who refuse to do so, it matters not however virtuously, yet are accused of discarding the claims of friendship by those persons whom they are unwilling to oblige; but they who dare to ask any thing of a friend, by their very request seem to imply that they would do any thing for the sake of that friend; by the complaining of such persons, not only are long-established intimacies put an end to, but endless animosities are engendered. All these many causes, like so many fatalities, are ever threatening friendship, so that he said, to escape them all, seemed to him a proof not merely of wisdom, but even of good fortune.

Wherefore let us first consider if you please, how far love ought to proceed in friendship. If Coriolanus had friends, were they bound to carry arms against their country with Coriolanus? Were their friends bound to support Viscellinus or Spurius Mælius when they aimed at the sovereignty? Nay, in the case of Tiberius Gracchus, when disturbing the commonwealth, we saw him totally abandoned by Quintus Tubero, and other friends of his own standing. But in the case of Caius Blossius, of Cumæ, the friend of our family, Scævola, when he had come to me (then attending upon the consuls Lænas and Rupilius in their council) to sue for pardon, he brought forward his plea, that he esteemed Tiberius Gracchus so highly that he thought it his duty to do whatever he wished. So I said, "What, even if he wished you to set fire to the capitol?" "He never would have thought of that," he replied. "But if he had?" "Then I would have complied." You see what an abominable speech: and by Hercules, he did so, and even worse than he said; for he did not follow the mad schemes of Tiberius Gracchus, but in fact headed them, and did not act as the accomplice of his violence, but even as the captain. Therefore in consequence of such rashness, being terrified by a new prosecution, he fled precipitately into Asia, joined the enemy, and atoned to the commonwealth by a punishment just and severe. It is no excuse therefore for a fault, that you committed it for a friend's sake; for since the belief in another's excellence was that which conciliated friendship, it is hard for friendship to continue when you have apostatized from virtue. Now if we shall lay it down as right, either to concede to friends whatever they wish, or to obtain from them whatever we wish, we must have indeed consummate wisdom, if such a course leads to no vice. But we are speaking of those friends who are before our eyes, whom we see around us, or else whom we know by report, and with whom every-day life is familiar; from that class we must take our instances, and above all, from those who make the nearest approaches to wisdom. We see that Papus Æmilius was the intimate friend of Caius Lucinus (so we have learned from our fathers); that they were twice consuls together, and colleagues in the censorship; and that at the same time Marcus Curius and Titus Coruncanius were most intimate with them and with each other, is a matter of history, and therefore we can not even suspect that any one of these ever asked his friend anything that was contrary to their honor, their oath, and the interest of the state: for what reason is there for making such a remark about men like them? I am convinced had any of them made the request he would not have obtained it, for they were men of the purest principle; besides, it would be equally as wrong to agree to any such request when made, as to make it. And yet Caius Carbo and Caius Cato both took the part of Tiberius Gracchus, as did his brother Caius, at that time by no means an agitator, but now one of the most violent.

Let this law therefore be established in friendship, viz., that we should neither ask things that are improper nor grant them when asked; for it is a disgraceful apology, and by no means to be admitted, as well in the case of other offenses, as when any one avows he has acted against the state for the sake of a friend. For we are placed, O Fannius and Scævola, in such a position that we ought to see from a distance the future calamities of the commonwealth; for the practice of our ancestors has already in some respect swerved from its career and course. Tiberius Gracchus has endeavored to obtain the sovereignty, or rather he reigned for a few months. Had the Roman people ever heard or witnessed anything similar? Even after his death his friends and relations maintained his cause; and what malice they exercised against Publius Scipio I can not relate without tears; for, owing to the recent punishment of Tiberius Gracchus, we withstood Carbo by whatever means we could. And concerning the tribuneship of Caius Gracchus, what we have to expect I have no disposition to anticipate; still the movement is creeping on, and when once it has begun, it rushes with increasing precipitation to destruction; for already you have seen, with regard to the ballot, what great mischief has been caused—first, by the Gabinian law, and two years after by the Cassian; for already I fancy I see the people separated from the senate, and the most important measures carried at the caprice of the mob; far more people will learn how such things may be done than how they may be resisted. Wherefore do I say this? Because without allies no one attempts any thing of the kind; therefore this should be pressed on all good men, that if inadvertently they should have fallen unawares into friendships of that character, they must think themselves bound in such a manner that they must not desert their friends when doing wrong in any important matter; at the same time, punishment should be enacted against the wicked; and not less severe for those who have followed another than for those who have been themselves the leaders of the wickedness. Who was more illustrious in Greece than Themistocles? Who more powerful? And when he, as general in the Persian war, had freed Greece from slavery, and through unpopularity had been driven into exile, he could not endure the injustice of his ungrateful country, which he ought to have borne. He acted the same part as Coriolanus had done among us twenty years before. No one was found to support these men against their country; accordingly, they both committed suicide.

Wherefore such a combination with wicked men not only must not be sheltered under the excuse of friendship, but should rather be visited with every kind of punishments; so that no one may think it permitted to him to follow a friend, even when waging war against his country. And as matters have begun to proceed, I know not whether that will not some day occur. To me, however, it is no less a cause of anxiety in what state the republic shall be after my death than in what state it is at this day.

Let this, therefore, be established as a primary law concerning friendship, that we expect from our friends only what is honorable, and for our friends' sake do what is honorable; that we should not wait till we are asked; that zeal be ever ready, and reluctance far from us; but that we take pleasure in freely giving our advice; that in our friendship the influence of our friends, when they give good advice, should have great weight; and that this be employed to admonish not only candidly, but even severely, if the case shall require, and that we give heed to it when so employed; for, as to certain persons, whom I understand to have been esteemed wise men in Greece, I am of opinion that some strange notions were entertained by them; but there is nothing which they do not follow up with too great subtlety; among the rest, that excessive friendships should be avoided, lest it should be necessary for one to feel anxiety for many;

that every one has enough, and more than enough, of
his own affairs; that to be needlessly implicated in those
of other people is vexatious; that it was most con-
venient to hold the reins of friendship as loose as possible, so as either to tighten or slacken them when you
please: for they argue that the main point toward a
happy life is freedom from care, which the mind can
not enjoy if one man be, as it were, in travail for others. Nay, they tell us that some are accustomed to
declare, still more unfeelingly (a topic which I have
briefly touched upon just above), that friendships
should be cultivated for the purpose of protection and
assistance, and not for kind feeling or affection; and
therefore the less a man possesses of independence and
of strength, in the same degree he most earnestly desires friendships; that thence it arises that women seek
the support of friendship more than men, and the poor
more than the rich, and persons in distress rather than
those who are considered prosperous. Admirable phil-
osophy! for they seem to take away the sun from the
world who withdraw friendship from life; for we receive nothing better from the immortal gods, nothing
more delightful; for what is this freedom from care?
—in appearances, indeed, flattering; but, in many cases
in reality to be disdained. Nor is it reasonable to refuse to undertake any honorable matter or action lest
you should be anxious, or to lay it aside when under-

taken; for if we fly from care, we must fly from virtue
also; for it is impossible that she can, without some degree of distress, feel contempt and detestation for qualities opposed to herself; just as kind-heartedness for
malice, temperance for profligacy, and bravery for
cowardice. Accordingly, you see that upright men are
most distressed by unjust actions; the brave with the
cowardly; the virtuous with the profligate; and, therefore, this is the characteristic of a well-regulated mind,
both to be well pleased with what is excellent, and to
be distressed with what is contrary. Wherefore, if
trouble of mind befall a wise man (and assuredly it
will, unless we suppose that all humanity is extirpated
from his mind), what reason is there why we should
altogether remove friendship from life, lest because of
it we should take upon ourselves some troubles? for what
difference is there (setting the emotions of the mind
aside), I do not say between a man and a beast, but between a man and a stone, or log, or anything of that
kind? For they do not deserve to be listened to, who
would have virtue to be callous, and made of iron, as it
were; which indeed is, as in other matters, so in friendship also, tender and susceptible; so that friends are
loosened, as it were, by happy events, and drawn together by distresses.

Wherefore the anxiety which has often to be felt for
a friend, is not of such force that it should remove

friendship from the world, any more than that the virtues, because they bring with them certain cares and troubles, should therefore be discarded. For when it produces friendship (as I said above), should any indication of virtue shine forth, to which a congenial mind may attach and unite itself—when this happens, affection must necessarily arise. For what is so unmeaning as to take delight in many vain things, such as preferments, glory, magnificent buildings, clothing and adornment of the body; and not to take an extreme delight in a soul endued with virtue, in such a soul as can either love, or (so to speak) love in return? for there is nothing more delightful than the repayment of kindness, and the interchange of devotedness and good offices. Now, if we add this, which may with propriety be added, that there is nothing which so allures and draws any object to itself as congeniality does friendship; it will, of course, be admitted as true that the good must love the good, and unite them to themselves, just as if connected by relationship and nature; for nothing is more apt to seek and seize on its like than nature. Wherefore this certainly is clear, Fannius and Scævola, (in my opinion), that among the good a liking for the good is, as it were, inevitable; and this indeed is appointed by nature herself as the very fountain of friendship. But the same kind disposition belongs also to the multitude; for virtue is not inhuman, or cruel, or haughty, since she is accustomed to protect even whole nations, and to adopt the best measures for their welfare, which assuredly she would not do did she shrink from the affection of the vulgar. And to myself, indeed, those who form friendships with a view to advantage, seem to do away with its most endearing bond; for it is not so much the advantage obtained through a friend as the mere love of that friend, which delights; and then only what has proceeded from a friend becomes delightful if it has proceeded from zealous affection; and that friendship should be cultivated from a sense of necessity, is so far from being the case that those who, being endowed with power and wealth, and especially with virtue (in which is the strongest support of friendship), have least need of another, are most liberal and generous. Yet I am not sure whether it is requisite that friends should never stand in any need; for wherein would any devotedness of mine to him have been exerted if Scipio had never stood in need of my advice or assistance at home or abroad? Wherefore friendship has not followed upon advantage, but advantage on friendship.

Persons, therefore, who are wallowing in indulgence, will not need to be listened to if ever they shall descant upon friendship, which they have known neither by experience nor by theory. For who is there, by the faith of gods and men, who would desire, on the condition of his loving no one, and himself being loved by none, to roll in affluence, and live in a superfluity of all things? For this is the life of tyrants, in which undoubtedly there can be no confidence, no affection, no steady dependence on attachment; all is perpetually mistrust and disquietude—there is no room for friendship. For who can love either him whom he fears, or him by whom he thinks he himself is feared? Yet are they courted, solely in hypocrisy, for a time; because, if perchance (as it frequently happens) they have been brought low, then it is perceived how destitute they were of friends. And this, they say, Tarquin expressed; that when going into exile, he found out whom he had as faithful friends, and whom unfaithful ones, since then he could no longer show gratitude to either party; although I wonder that, with such haughtiness and impatience of temper, he could find one at all. And as the character of the individual whom I have mentioned could not obtain true friends, so the riches of many men of rank exclude all faithful friendship; for not only is fortune blind herself, but she commonly renders blind those whom she embraces. Accordingly, such persons are commonly puffed up with pride and insolence, nor can any thing be found more intolerable than a fortunate fool. And thus, indeed, one may observe, that those who before were of agreeable character, by military command, by preferment, by prosperity, are changed, and old friend-

ships are despised by them, and new ones cherished.
For what can be more foolish than, when men are possessed of great influence by their wealth, power, and
resources, to procure other things which are procured
by money—horses, slaves, rich apparel, costly vases—
and not to procure friends, the most valuable and fairest
furniture of life, if I may so speak; for while they are
procuring those things, they know not for whom they
are procuring them, nor for whose sake they are labor-
ing. For every one of these things belongs to him who
is most powerful, whereas the possession of his friendships is preserved to every one steadfast and secure; so
that if those things are preserved which are, as it were,
the gifts of fortune, yet a life unadorned and abandoned
by friends can not possibly be happy. But on this head
enough.

But it is required to lay down what limits there are
in friendship, and, as it were, what bounds of loving,
concerning which I see three opinions held, of none of
which I approve:—the first that we should be affected
toward a friend in the same manner as toward ourselves;
the second, that our good-will toward our friends should
exactly and equally answer to their good-will toward us;
the third, that at whatever value a man sets himself, at
the same he should be estimated by his friends. To
none of these three opinions do I entirely assent. For
the first one is not true, that as a man feels toward him-

self so he should be disposed toward his friend. For
how many things, which for our own sake we should
never do, do we perform for the sake of our friends?
To ask favors of unworthy persons, to supplicate them,
to inveigh bitterly against any one, and to accuse him
with great vehemence, which in our own cases cannot
be done creditably, in the case of our friends are most
honorably done; and there are many cases in which
good men subtract many things from their own interests,
or allow them to be subtracted, that their friends, rather
than themselves, may enjoy them. The second opinion
is that which limits friendship to an equality of kind
actions and kind wishes; this is indeed to reduce friendship to figures too minutely and penuriously, so that
there may be a balance of received and paid. True
friendship seems to be far too rich and affluent for that,
and not to observe, narrowly, lest it should pay more
than it receives: nor need it be feared lest any thing
should be lost or fall to the ground, or lest more than
what is fair should be accumulated on the side of friendship. But the third limitation is most detestable, that
at whatever value a man sets on himself, at that value
he should be estimated by his friends; for often, in certain persons, either their spirit is too humble, or their
hope of improving their condition too desponding; it is
not, therefore, the part of a friend to be toward him
what he is to himself; but rather to use every effort, and

to contrive to cheer the prostrate spirit of his friend, and to encourage better hopes and thoughts. Therefore, I must lay down some other limit of true friendship, as soon as I shall have stated what Scipio was accustomed, above all things, to reprehend. He used to declare that no speech could be found more hostile to friendship, than his who had said that a man ought so to love as if one day he would come to hate. Nor, indeed, could he be induced to believe that this, as was supposed, was said by Bias, who was considered one of the seven wise men; but that it was the opinion of some wicked or ambitious man, or one who sought to bring everything under his own power. For in what manner can any one be a friend to him to whom he thinks he may possibly become an enemy? Moreover it will follow that he desires and wishes his friend to do wrong as often as possible, that he may afford him, as it were, so many handles for reproach. And, again, at the right conduct and advantage of his friends he will necessarily be tormented, grieved, and jealous. Wherefore this precept, to whomsoever it belongs, is powerful only for the destruction of friendship. This, rather, should have been the precept, that we should employ such carefulness in forming our friendships, that we should not any time begin to love the man whom we could ever possibly hate. Moreover, if we have been but unfortunate in our selection, Scipio was of opinion that this should be submitted to, rather than that a time of alienation should ever be contemplated.

I think, therefore, we must adopt these limitations, that when the character of friends is correct, then there should be a community between them of all things, of purpose and of will, without any exception; so that, even if by any chance it has happened that the less honorable wishes of our friends have to be forwarded, in which either their life is concerned, or their reputation, then you may decline a little from the straight path, provided only extreme infamy do not follow; for there is a point to which indulgence may be granted to friendship; yet reputation must not be disregarded; nor ought we to esteem the good-will of our fellow-countrymen as an engine of small value in the administration of the state, although to seek it by fawning and flattering is mean indeed; yet virtue, on which affection is consequent, should by no means be rejected. But frequently (for I return to Scipio, the whole of whose discourse was concerning friendship) he used to complain, that in all other things men were comparatively careful; so that every man could tell how many goats or how many sheep he possessed, yet how many friends he had he could not tell; and in procuring the former, men employed carefulness, while in selecting their friends they were negligent, nor had they, as it were, any signs or marks by which they determined who were suited for friendship. The steadfast, then, and the steady, and the consistent, are to be selected, of which class of persons there is a great scarcity; and, in truth, it is difficult for any one to judge, unless after he is experienced. Now the trial must be made in actual friendship; thus friendship outstrips judgment, and removes the power of making experiments. It is the part, therefore, of a prudent man, to check the impetus of his kindly feeling as he would his chariot, that we may have our friendships, like our horses, fully proved, when the character of our friends has been in some measure tested. Of some, it is often discovered in small sums of money how void of worth they are. Some, whom a small sum of money could not influence, are discovered in the case of a large one. But, even if some shall be found who think it sordid to prefer money to friendship, where should we find those who do not place above friendship high dignities, magistracies, military command, civil authorities and influence? so that, when on the one side these objects have been proposed, and the claim of friendship on the other, they would not far prefer the former. For nature is too weak to despise the possession of power; for, even if they have attained it by the slighting of friendship, they think the act will be thrown into the shade, because friendship was not overlooked without strong grounds. Therefore real friendships are found with most difficulty among those who are invested with high offices, or in business of the state. For where can you find the man who would prefer his friend's advancement to his own? And why? For to pass over these matters, how grievous, how impracticable to most men, does participation in afflictions appear! to which it is not easy to find the man who will descend. Although Ennius truly says, "A sure friend is discerned in an unsure matter," yet these two charges of inconstancy and of weakness condemn most men; either in their prosperity they despise a friend, or in his troubles they desert him.

He who, therefore, shall have shown himself in both cases as regards friendship, worthy, consistent and steadfast, such a one we ought to esteem of a class of persons extremely rare, nay, almost godlike. Now, the foundation of that steadfastness and constancy, which we seek in friendship, is sincerity. For nothing is steadfast which is insincere. Besides, it is right that one should be chosen who is frank and good-natured, and congenial in his sentiments; one, in fact, who is influenced by the same motives; all which qualities have a tendency to create sincerity. For it is impossible for a wily and tortuous disposition to be sincere. Nor in truth can the man who has no sympathy from nature, and who is not moved by the same considerations, be either attached or steady. To the same requisites must be added that he shall neither take delight in bringing forward charges, nor believe them when they arise; all which causes belong to that consistent principle, of which now for some time I have been treating. Thus the remark is true which I made at first, that friendship can only exist among the good; for it is the part of a good man (whom at the same time we may call a wise man), to observe these two rules in friendship: first, that there shall be nothing pretended or simulated (for even to hate openly better becomes the ingenuous man than by his looks to conceal his sentiments); in the next place, that not only does he repel charges when brought (against his friends) by any one, but is not himself suspicious, ever fancying that some infidelity has been committed by his friend. To all this there should be added a certain suavity of conversation and manners, affording, as it does, no inconsiderable zest to friendship. Now solemnity and gravity on all occasions, certainly, carry with them dignity; but friendship ought to be easier and more free and more pleasant, and tending more to every kind of politeness and good nature.

But there arises on this subject a somewhat difficult question; whether ever new friends, if deserving friendship, are to be preferred to old ones, just as we are wont to prefer young colts to old horses? a perplexity unworthy of a man; for there ought to be no satiety of friendship as of other things; everything which is oldest (as those wines which bear age well) ought to be sweetest; and that is true which is sometimes said, "many bushels of salt must be eaten together," before the duty of friendship can be fulfilled. But new friendships, if they afford a hope that, as in the case of plants which never disappoint, fruits shall appear, such are not to be rejected; yet the old one must be preserved in its proper place, for the power of age and custom is exceedingly great; besides, in the very case of the horse, which I just mentioned, if there is no impediment, there is no one who does not more pleasurably use that to which he is accustomed than one unbroken and strange to him; and habit asserts its power, and habit prevails, not only in the case of this, which is animate, but also in the cases of those things which are inanimate, since we take delight in the very mountainous or woody scenery among which we have long dwelt. But it is of the greatest importance in friendship that the superior should be on an equality with the inferior. For there often are instances of superiority, as was the case with Scipio, one, so to speak, of our own herd. He never ranked himself above Philus, or Rupilius, or Mummius, or other friends of an inferior grade. But his brother, Quintus Maximus, a distinguished man, though by no means equal to himself, simply because he was the elder, he treated as his superior, and he wished all his friends should receive additional dignity through him. And this conduct should be adopted and imitated by all, so that if they have attained to any excellence in worth, genius or fortune, they should communicate them with their friends, and share them with their connections; so that if men have been born of humble parentage, or if they have kinsmen less powerful than themselves, either in mind or in fortune, they should increase the consequence of such persons, and be to them a source of credit and of dignity; as in works of fiction, they who for some time, through ignorance of their origin and descent, have been in a state of servitude, when they have been discovered and found out to be the sons of gods or kings, yet retain their affection for the shepherds, whom for many years they looked upon as their parents. And this assuredly is much rather to be observed in the case of parents that are real and undoubted. For the fruit of talent, and worth, and every excellence, is gathered most fully when it is bestowed on every one most nearly connected with us.

As therefore those who are superior in the connection of friendship and of union ought to put themselves on a level with their inferiors, so ought the inferiors not to grieve that they are surpassed by their friends, either in genius, or fortune, or rank; whereas most of them are always either complaining of something, or even breaking out into reproaches; and so much the more if they think they have any thing which they can say was done by them in an obliging and friendly manner with some exertion on their part. A disgusting set of people assuredly they are who are ever reproaching you with their services; which the man on whom they are conferred ought indeed to remember, but he who conferred them ought not to call them to mind. Wherefore, as those who are superior ought in the exercise of friendship to condescend, so, in a measure, they ought to raise up their inferiors. For there are some persons who render friendships with them annoying, while they fancy they are slighted; this does not commonly happen except to those who think themselves liable to be slighted; and from this belief they require to be relieved, not only by your professions, but by your actions. Now, first of all, so much advantage is to be bestowed on each as you yourself can produce; and in the next place, as much as he whom you love and assist can bear; for you could not, however eminent you might be, bring all your friends to the very highest honor; just as Scipio had power to make Publius Rutulius consul, but could not do the same for his brother Lucius; indeed, even if you have the power to confer what you please on another, yet you must consider what he can bear. On the whole, those connections only can be considered as friendships, when both the dispositions and age have been established and matured. Nor, when persons have been in early life attached to hunting or tennis, are they bound to make intimates of those whom at that time they loved, as being endowed with the same taste: for on that principle, our nurses and the tutors of our childhood, by right of priority, will claim the greatest part of our affection; who, indeed, should not be neglected, but possess our regard in some other manner: otherwise friendships could not continue steadfast. For dissimilar habits and dissimilar pursuits ensue; the dissimilarity of which severs friendships: it is for no other cause that the good can not be friends of the worthless, or the worthless of the good; but that there is between them the greatest difference that can subsist of characters and pursuits. For in friendships this precept may be properly laid down, not to let ill-regulated affection (as often is the case) thwart and impede the great usefulness of friends; nor in truth (to revert to fiction), could Neoptolemus have taken Troy if he had been inclined to listen to Lycomedes, with whom he had been brought up, when with many tears he sought to prevent his journey: and often important occasions arise, so that you must bid farewell to your friends; and he who would hinder them, because he can not easily bear the regret for their loss, such an one is both weak and effeminate by nature, and on that ground unjust in his friendship.

And in every case it is necessary to consider, both what you would ask of a friend, and what favor you would permit to be obtained from yourself.

There is a kind of calamity also, sometimes inevitable, in the discarding of friendships. For at length our discourse descends, from the intimacies of the wise, to ordinary friendships. The faults of friends often break out as well on the friends themselves as on strangers; and yet the disgrace of such persons must redound to their friends: such friendships therefore must be dissolved by the intermission of intercourse, and (as I have heard Cato say) should be ripped rather than rent; unless some intolerable sense of wrong has been kindled, so that it is neither right, nor creditable, nor possible that an estrangement and separation should not take place immediately. But if any change of character or pursuits (as commonly happens) shall have taken place, or quarrel arisen with respect to political parties (for I speak now, as I observed a little before, not of the friendships of the wise but of such as are ordinary), we should have to be cautious, lest not only friendships be found to be laid aside, but even animosity to have been incurred; for nothing can be more disgraceful than to be at war with him with whom you have lived on terms of friendship. From his friendship with Quintus Pompey, Scipio had withdrawn himself on my account (as you know); moreover, on account of the dissension which existed in the republic, he was estranged from my colleague Metellus; on both occasions he acted with dignity and decision, and with an offended but not bitter feeling. Wherefore, in the first place, pains must be taken that there be no alienation of friends; but if aught of the kind shall have occurred, that that friendship should seem rather to have died away than to have been violently destroyed. In truth we must take care lest friendship turn into bitter hostilities; from which quarrels, hard language, and insults are produced, and yet if they shall be bearable, they must be borne; and thus much honor should be paid to an old friendship, that he shall be in fault who inflicts the injury, and not he who suffers it. On the whole, against all such faults and inconveniences there is one precaution and one provision, that we should not begin to love too hastily, nor love unworthy persons. Now they are worthy of friendship in whom there exists a reason why they should be loved; a rare class (for in truth all that is excellent is rare), nor is aught more difficult than to find any thing which in every respect is perfect of its kind: but most men recognize nothing as good in human affairs but what is profitable; and with their friends as with cattle, they love those most especially from whom they hope they will receive most advantage; and thus they are destitute of that most beautiful and most natural friendship, which is desirable for itself and of itself; nor do they exemplify to themselves what and how powerful this quality of friendship is. For every one loves himself, not that he may exact from himself some reward of his affection, but that, for his own sake, every one is dear to himself. And unless this same principle be transferred to friendship, a true friend will never be found; for such an one is, as it were, a second self. Now, if this is apparent in beasts, birds, fishes, creatures of the field, tame and wild, that first they love themselves (for the principle is alike born with every living thing); in the next place that they seek out and desire some creatures of the same species to which they may unite themselves, and do this with desire, and with a kind of resemblance to human love; how much more naturally does this take place in man by nature, who not only loves himself, but seeks for another whose soul he may so mingle with his own, as almost to create one person out of two?

Yet most men, perversely, not to say shamelessly, desire to have a friend, such as they themselves are unable to be: and allowances which they themselves make not for their friends, they require from them. Now, the fair thing is, first that a man himself should be good, and then that he should seek another like to himself. Among such persons, there may be established that solidity of friendship which I have long been treating on; when men are united by benevolent feeling, they will first of all master those passions to which others

are slaves; next, they will take pleasure in equity and
justice, and the one will undertake every thing for the
other; nor will the one ever ask of the other any thing
but what is honorable and right: nor will they only
mutually regard and love each other, but even have a
feeling of respect; for he removes the greatest ornament
of friendship who takes away from it respect. Accordingly, there is a pernicious error in those who think that
a free indulgence in all lusts and sins is extended in
friendship. Friendship was given us by nature as the
handmaid of virtues, and not as the companion of our
vices: that since, alone and unaided, virtue could not
arrive at the highest attainments, she might be able to
do so when united and associated with another; and if such
a society between any persons either exists or has existed,
or is likely to do so, their companionship is to be esteemed, in respect of the chief good in life, most excellent and most happy. This, I say, is that association in
which all things exist which men deem worthy the pursuit—reputation, high esteem, peace of mind, and cheerfulness; so that where these blessings are present, life is
happy, and without these can not be so. And whereas
this is the best and highest of objects, if we would gain
it, attention must be paid to virtue; without which we
can neither obtain friendship nor any thing worthy of
pursuit: indeed, should this be disregarded, they who
think they possess friends, too late find that they are

mistaken, when some grievous misfortune compels them
to make the trial.   Wherefore (for I must say it again
and again) when you have formed your judgment, then
it behooves you to give your affections; and not when
you have given your affections, then to form the judgment; but while in many cases we suffer for our care-
lessness, so especially in choosing and cultivating friends;
for we adopt a preposterous plan, and set about doing
what has been already done, which we are forbidden by
the old proverb to do.   For, being entangled on every
side, either by daily intercourse or else by kind offices,
suddenly, in the middle of our course, on some offense
arising, we break off our friendships altogether.

Wherefore so much the more is this great negligence
to be blamed in a matter of the highest necessity.   For
friendship is the only point in human affairs, concerning the benefit of which all with one voice agree; although by many virtue herself is despised, and is said
to be a mere bragging and ostentation.   Many persons despise riches; for, being content with a little,
moderate food and a moderate style of living delights them; as to high offices, in truth, with the ambitious desire of which some men are inflamed, how
many men so completely disregard them that they think
nothing is more vain and more trifling; and likewise
there are those who reckon as nothing other things
which to some men seem worthy of admiration; con-

cerning friendship, all to a man have the same opinion. Those who have devoted themselves to political affairs, and those who find pleasure in knowledge and learning, and those who transact their own affairs at their leisure, and lastly, those who have given themselves wholly up to pleasure, feel that without friendship life is nothing, at least if they are inclined in any degree to live respectably; for somehow or other, friendship entwines itself with the life of all men, nor does it suffer any mode of spending our life to be independent of itself. Moreover, if there is any one of such ferocity and brutality of nature that he shuns and hates the intercourse of mankind, such as we have heard that one Timon was at Athens; yet even he can not possibly help looking out for some one on whom he may disgorge the venom of his ill-nature. And this would be most clearly decided if something of this kind could happen—that some god should remove us from the crowded society of men, and place us somewhere in solitude, and there supplying us with abundance and plenty of all things which nature requires, yet should take from us altogether the opportunity of seeing a human being, who would then be so insensible that he could endure such a life, and from whom would not solitude take away the enjoyment of all pleasure? Accordingly, there is truth in that which I have heard our old men relate to have been commonly said by Archytas of Tarentum, and I think heard by them from others their elders, that if any one could have ascended to the sky and surveyed the structure of the universe, and the beauty of the stars, that such admiration would be insipid to him; and yet it would be most delightful if he had some one to whom he might describe it. Thus nature loves nothing solitary, and always reaches out to something as a support, which ever in the sincerest friend is most delightful.

But while nature declares by so many indications what she likes, seeks after, and requires, yet we turn, I know not how, a deaf ear, nor do we listen to those admonitions which we receive from her. For the intercourse of friendship is various and manifold, and many occasions are presented of suspicion and offense, which it is the part of a wise man sometimes to wink at, sometimes to make light of, or at others to endure. This one ground of offense must be mitigated in order that truth and sincerity in friendship may be preserved; for friends require to be advised and to be reproved; and such treatment ought to be taken in a friendly spirit when it is kindly meant. But somehow or other it is very true what my dear friend Terence says in his Andria: " Complaisance begets friends, but truth ill-will." Truth is grievous, if indeed ill-will arises from it, which is the bane of friendship. But complaisance is much more grievous, because it allows a friend to be precipitated into ruin by yielding to his faults. But

the greatest of all faults is chargeable on him who dis-
regards truth, and thus by complaisance is led into dis-
honesty. Accordingly, in managing this whole matter,
carefulness and diligence must be employed; first, that
our advice may be free from bitterness, and next, that
reproof may be unattended by insult; in our complaisance, however (since I gladly adopt the saying of
Terence), let there be a kindness of manner, let flattery,
however, the handmaid of vices, be far removed, since
it is not only unworthy of a friend, but even of a free
man; for you live after one fashion with a tyrant, after
another with a friend. Now where a man's ears are
shut against the truth, so that he can not hear the truth
from a friend, the welfare of such a one is to be de-
spaired of; for the following remark of Cato is shrewd,
as many of his are, "that bitter enemies deserve better
at the hands of some than those friends who seem
agreeable; that the former often speak the truth, the
latter never." And it is an absurd thing that those
who receive advice do not experience that annoyance
which they ought to feel, but feel that from which they
ought to be free; for they are not distressed because
they have done wrong, but take it amiss that they are
rebuked; whereas, on the contrary, they ought to be
sorry for their misconduct, and to be glad at its correction.

As, therefore, both to give and to receive advice is

the characteristic of true friendship, and that the one should perform his part with freedom but not harshly, and the other should receive it patiently and not with recrimination; so it should be considered that there is no greater bane to friendship than adulation, fawning, and flattery. For this vice should be branded under as many names as possible, being that of worthless and designing men, who say every thing with a view of pleasing, and nothing with regard to truth. Now while hypocrisy in all things is blamable (for it does away with all judgment of truth, and adulterates truth itself), so especially is it repugnant to friendship, for it destroys all truth, without which the name of friendship can avail nothing. For since the power of friendship consists in this, that one soul is as it were made of many, how could that take place if there should not be in any one a soul, one and the same always, but fickle, changeable, and manifold? For what can be so pliant, so inconsistent, as the soul of that man, who veers not only to the feelings and wishes, but even to the look and very nod of another. "Does any one say, 'No?' so do I; says any, 'Yes?' so do I: in a word, I have charged myself to assent to every thing," as the same Terence says; but he speaks in the character of Gnatho, and to select a friend of this character is an act of downright folly. And there are many like Gnatho, though his superiors in rank, fortune, and character; the flattery of such

people is offensive indeed, since respectability is associated with duplicity. Now a fawning friend may be
distinguished from a true one, and discerned by the em-
ployment of diligence, just as every thing which is
falsely colored and counterfeit, from what is genuine
and true. The assembly of the people, which consists
of the most ignorant persons, yet can decide what difference there is between the seeker after popular applause,
the flatterer and the worthless citizen, and one who is
consistent, dignified, and worthy. With what flatteries
did Curius Papirius lately insinuate himself into the ears
of the assembly, when he sought to pass an act to re-
elect the tribunes of the people? I opposed it. But I
say nothing of myself; I speak with greater pleasure
concerning Scipio. O immortal gods! what dignity
was his! what majesty in his speech! so that you might
readily pronounce him the leader of the Roman people,
and not their associate: but you were present, and the
speech is still extant: accordingly this act, meant to
please the people, was rejected by the votes of the people.
But, to return to myself, you remember when Quintus
Maximus, brother of Scipio, and Lucius Mancius were
consuls, how popular the sacredotal act of Caius Licinius
Crassus seemed to be; for the election of the college was
thereby transferred to the presentation of the people.
And he first commenced the practice of turning toward
the forum, and addressing the people. And yet regard

for the immortal gods, under my advocacy, gained an
easy triumph over his plausible address. Now this occurred in my prætorship, five years before I was consul;
so that that cause was supported rather by its own importance than by supreme influence.

Now, if upon the stage, that is, before the assembly,
where every advantage is given to fictions and imitations,
yet the truth prevails (if only it be set forth and illus-
trated), what ought to be the case in friendship, which
is measured according to simple truth? for in it (as the
saying is) ye see an open heart and show your own also;
you can have nothing faithful, nothing certain; and you
can not love or be loved, since you are uncertain how
far it is sincerely done. And yet that flattery, however
pernicious it be, can hurt no one but the man who receives it, and is most delighted with himself. Hence it
happens that he opens his ears widest to flatteries who is
a flatterer of himself, and takes the highest delight in
himself: no doubt virtue loves herself, for she is best
acquainted with herself, and is conscious how amiable
she is: but I am not speaking of virtue, but of a conceit
of virtue; for not so many desire to be endowed with
virtue itself, as to seem to be so. Flattery delights such
men: when conversation formed to their wishes is addressed to such persons, they think those deceitful ad-
dresses to be the evidence of their merits. This, therefore, is not friendship at all, when one party is unwill-

ing to hear the truth, and the other prepared to speak falsely. Nor would the flattery of parasites in comedies seem to us facetious, unless there were swaggering soldiers also. "Does then Thais pay me many thanks? It was enough to answer 'yes, many;' but he says 'infinite.'" The flatterer always exaggerates that which he, for whose pleasure he speaks, wishes to be great. Although the flattering falsehood may have influence with those who themselves allure and invite it; yet more steady and consistent persons require to be warned that they take care lest they are entrapped by such crafty flattery; for every one, except the man who is extremely obtuse, observes the person who openly employs adulation. But lest the crafty and insidious man should insinuate himself, you must be studiously on your guard; for he is not very easily recognized; seeing that he often flatters by opposing; and pretending that he quarrels, is fawning all the time, and at last surrenders himself, and allows himself to be beaten; so that he who has been deluded may fancy that he has seen further than the other; for what can be more disgraceful than to be deluded? And, lest this happen, we must be more cautious, as it is said in the Epiclerus, "To-day, above all the foolish old fellows of the comedy, you will have deceived me and played upon me in a most amusing manner." For this is the most foolish character of all in the plays, that of unthinking and credulous old men. But I know not how it is that my address, passing from the friendship of perfect men, that is of the wise (for I speak of that wisdom which seems within the reach of man), has digressed into frivolous friendships. Wherefore, let me return to that from which I set out, and bring these remarks at length to a conclusion.

It is virtue, virtue I say, Caius Fannius, and you, Quintus Mucius, that both wins friendship and preserves it; for in it is found the power of adapting one's self to circumstances, and also steadfastness and consistency; and when she has exalted herself and displayed her own effulgence, and hath beheld the same and recognized it in another, she moves toward it, and in her turn receives that which is in the other; from which is kindled love or friendship, for both derive their name from loving; for to love is nothing else than to be attached to the person whom you love, without any sense of want, without any advantage being sought; and yet advantage springs up of itself from friendship, even though you may not have pursued it. It was with kind feelings of this description that I, when young, was attached to those old men, Lucius Paullus, Marcus Cato, Caius Gallus, Publius Nasica, and Tiberius Gracchus, the father-in-law of our friend Scipio. This is even more strikingly obvious between persons of the same age as between me and Scipio, Lucius Furius, Publius Rupilius and Spurius Mummius; and now in turn, in my old age,

I repose in the attachment of younger men, as in yours and that of Quintus Tubero; nay, I even take delight in the familiarity of some that are very young, of Publius Rutilius and Aulius Virginius. And since the course of our life and nature is so directed that a new period is ever arising, it is especially to be wished that with those comrades with whom you set out, as it were, from the starting, with the same you may, as they say, arrive at the goal. But since human affairs are frail and fleeting, some persons must ever be sought for whom we may love, and by whom we may be loved; for when affection and kind feeling are done away with, all cheerfulness likewise is banished from existence. To me, indeed, though he was suddenly snatched away, Scipio still lives, and will always live; for I love the virtue of that man, and that worth is not yet extinguished; and not before my eyes only is it presented, who ever had it in possession, but even with posterity it will be illustrious and renowned; for never shall any undertake any high achievements with spirit and hope, without feeling that the memory and the character of that man should be placed before him. Assuredly, of all things that either fortune or nature has bestowed on me, I have none which I can compare with the friendship of Scipio. In it I had concurrence in politics, and in it advice for my private affairs. In it, also, I possessed a repose replete with pleasure. Never in the slightest degree did I of-fend him, at least so far as I was aware; never did I myself hear a word from him that I was unwilling to hear; we had one house between us, the same food, and that common to both; and not only service abroad, but even our traveling and visits to the country were in common. For what need I say of our constant pursuits of knowledge and learning, in which, retired from the eyes of the world, we spent all our leisure time? Now, if the recollection and memory of these things had died along with him, I could in no wise have borne the loss of that most intimate and affectionate friend; but these things have not perished, yea, they are rather cherished and improved by reflection and memory; and even if I were altogether bereft of them, yet would age itself bring me much comfort, for I can not now very long suffer these regrets. Now all afflictions, if brief, ought to be tolerable, howsoever great they may be. Such are the remarks I had to make on friendship. But as for you, I exhort you to lay the foundations of virtue, without which friendship can not exist, in such a manner that, with this one exception, you may consider that nothing in the world is more excellent than friendship.

OF FRIENDSHIP

BY

FRANCIS BACON

"If you have a friend worth loving, love him. Yes, and let him know that you love him ere life's evening tinge his brow with sunset glow. Why should good words ne'er be said of a friend 'till he is dead?"

"Good books, like intimate friends, should be few, but well chosen.

OF FRIENDSHIP.

It had been hard for him that spake it to have put more truth and untruth together in few words than in that speech: "Whosoever is delighted in solitude is either a wild beast or a god." For it is most true that a natural and secret hatred and aversation towards society, in any man, hath somewhat of the savage beast; but it is most untrue that it should have any character at all of the divine nature, except it proceed, not out of a pleasure in solitude, but out of a love and desire to sequester a man's self for a higher conversation, such as is found to have been falsely and feignedly in some of the heathen, as Epimenides the Candian, Numa the Roman, Empedocles the Sicilian, and Apollonius of Tyana; and truly and really in divers of the ancient hermits and holy fathers of the Church.

But little do men perceive what solitude is, and how far it extendeth. For a crowd is not company, and faces are but a gallery of pictures, and talk but a tinkling cymbal where there is no love. The Latin adage meeteth with it a little: *Magna civitas, magna solitudo;* because in a great town friends are scattered, so that there is not that fellowship for the most part which is in less neighbor-

*A great city is a great solitude.

hoods. But we may go further, and affirm most truly, that it is a mere and miserable solitude to want true friends, without which the world is but a wilderness; and even in this sense also of solitude, whosoever in the frame of his nature and affections is unfit for friendship, he taketh it of the beast and not from humanity.

A principal fruit of friendship is the ease and discharge of the fullness and swellings of the heart, which passions of all kinds do cause and induce. We know diseases of stoppings and suffocations are the most dangerous in the body; and it is not much otherwise in the mind. You may take sarza to open the liver; steel to open the spleen; flowers of sulphur for the lungs; castoreum for the brain; but no receipt openeth the heart but a true friend, to whom you may impart griefs, joys, fears, hopes, suspicions, counsels, and whatsoever lieth upon the heart to oppress it, in a kind of civil shrift or confession.

It is a strange thing to observe how high a rate great kings and monarchs do set upon this fruit of friendship whereof we speak; so great, as they purchase it many times at the hazard of their own safety and greatness. For princes, in regard of the distance of their fortune from that of their subjects and servants, cannot gather this fruit except (to make themselves capable thereof) they raise some persons to be, as it were, companions and almost equals to themselves, which many times

sorteth to inconvenience. The modern languages give unto such persons the name of favorites, or privadoes, as if it were matter of grace or conversation. But the Roman name attaineth the true use and cause thereof; naming them *participes curarum;* for it is that which tieth the knot. And we see plainly that this hath been done, not by weak and passionate princes only, but by the wisest and most politic that ever reigned, who have oftentimes joined to themselves some of their servants, whom both themselves have called friends and allowed others likewise to call them in the same manner, using the word which is received between private men.

L. Sylla, when he commanded Rome, raised Pompey (after surnamed the Great) to that height that Pompey vaunted himself for Sylla's overmatch. For when he had carried the consulship for a friend of his, against the pursuit of Sylla, and that Sylla did a little resent thereat, and began to speak great, Pompey turned upon him again, and in effect bade him be quiet: "For that more men adored the sun rising than the sun setting." With Julius Cæsar, Decimus Brutus had obtained that interest, as he set him down in his testament for heir in remainder, after his nephew. And this was the man that had power with him to draw him forth to his death; for when Cæsar would have discharged the Senate, in regard of some ill presages, and specially a dream of

*Sharers in cares.

Calpurnia, this man lifted him gently by the arm out of his chair, telling him he hoped he would not dismiss the Senate till his wife had dreamt a better dream. And it seemeth his favor was so great, as Antonius, in a letter, which is recited verbatim in one of Cicero's Philippics; calleth him *venefica* (witch), as if he had enchanted Cæsar. Augustus raised Agrippa, though of mean birth, to that height as when he consulted with Mæcenas about the marriage of his daughter Julia, Mæcenas took the liberty to tell him that he must either marry his daughter to Agrippa or take away his life; there was no third way, he had made him so great. With Tiberius Cæsar, Sejanus had ascended to that height as they two were termed and reckoned as a pair of friends. Tiberius, in a letter to him saith, *Hæc pro amicitia nostra non occultavi;* and the whole Senate dedicated an altar to Friendship, as to a goddess, in respect of the great dearness of friendship between them two. The like, or more, was between Septimius Severus and Plautianus; for he forced his eldest son to marry the daughter of Plautianus, and would often maintain Plautianus in doing affronts to his son, and did write also in a letter to the Senate by these words, "I love the man so well as I wish he may overlive me." Now, if these princes had been as a Trajan or a Marcus Aurelius, a man might have thought that this had proceeded of an

---

*These things on account of our friendship I have not concealed.

abundant goodness of nature; but being men so wise, of such strength and severity of mind, and so extreme lovers of themselves, as all these were, it proveth most plainly that they found their own felicity, though as great as ever happened to mortal men, but as an half-piece, except they might have a friend to make it entire; and yet, which is more, they were princes that had wives, sons, nephews; and yet all these could not supply the comfort of friendship.

It is not to be forgotten what Commineus observeth of his first master, Duke Charles the Hardy—namely, that he would communicate his secrets with none; and, least of all those secrets which troubled him most. Whereupon he goeth on, and saith, that towards his latter time, "That closeness did impair and a little perish his understanding." Surely, Commineus might have made the same judgment also, if it had pleased him, of his second master, Lewis the Eleventh, whose closeness was indeed his tormentor. The parable of Pythagoras is dark, but true: *Cor ne edito* (Eat not the heart). Certainly, if a man would give it a hard phrase, those that want friends to open themselves unto are cannibals of their own hearts. But one thing is most admirable (wherewith I will conclude this first fruit of friendship), which is, that this communicating of a man's self to his friend works two contrary effects; for it redoubleth joys, and cutteth griefs in halves. For there is no man that imparteth his joys to his friend, but he joyeth the more; and no man that imparteth his griefs to his friend, but he grieveth the less. So that it is, in truth, of operation upon a man's mind of like virtue, as the alchymists use to attribute to their stone, for man's body, that it worketh all contrary effects, but still to the good and benefit of nature. But yet, without praying in aid of alchemists, there is a manifest image of this in the ordinary course of nature. For, in bodies, union strengtheneth and cherisheth any natural action; and, on the other side, weakeneth and dulleth any violent impression: and even so it is of minds.

The second fruit of friendship is healthful and sovereign for the understanding, as the first is for the affections. For friendship maketh indeed a fair day in the affections from storms and tempests; but it maketh daylight in the understanding, out of darkness and confusion of thoughts. Neither is this to be understood only of faithful counsel, which a man receiveth from his friend; but before you come to that, certain it is that whosoever hath his mind fraught with many thoughts, his wits and understanding do clarify and break up in the communicating and discoursing with another, he tosseth his thoughts more easily; he marshalleth them more orderly; he seeth how they look when they are turned into words. Finally, he waxeth wiser than himself, and that more by an hour's discourse than by a day's meditation. It was well said by Themistocles to the king of Persia, "That speech was like cloth of Arras, opened, and put abroad, whereby the imagery doth appear in figure; whereas, in thoughts, they lie but as in packs." Neither is this second fruit of friendship, in opening the understanding, restrained only to such friends as are able to give a man counsel (they, indeed, are best); but even without that a man learneth of himself, and bringeth his own thoughts to light, and whetteth his wits as against a stone, which itself cuts not. In a word, a man were better relate himself to a statue or picture than to suffer his thoughts to pass in smother.

Add now, to make this second fruit of friendship complete, that other point, which lieth more open, and falleth within vulgar observation, which is faithful counsel from a friend. Heraclitus saith well in one of his enigmas: "Dry light is ever the best." And certain it is, that the light that a man receiveth by counsel from another is drier and purer than that which cometh from his own understanding and judgment, which is ever infused and drenched in his affections and customs. So as there is as much difference between the counsel that a friend giveth and that a man giveth himself as there is between the counsel of a friend and of a flatterer. For there is no such flatterer as is a man's self; and there is no such remedy against flattery of a man's self as the liberty of a friend. Counsel is of two sorts; the one concerning manners, the other concerning business. For the first, the best preservative to keep the mind in health is the faithful admonition of a friend. The calling of a man's self to a strict account is a medicine sometime too piercing and corrosive. Reading good books of morality is a little flat and dead. Observing our faults in others is sometimes improper for our case. But the best receipt (best, I say, to work, and best to take), is the admonition of a friend.

It is a strange thing to behold what gross errors and extreme absurdities many, especially of the greater sort, do commit for want of a friend to tell them of them, to the great damage both of their fame and fortune. For, as St. James saith, they are as men "that look sometimes into a glass, and presently forget their own shape and favor." As for business, a man may think, if he will, that two eyes see no more than one; or that a gamester seeth always more than a looker-on; or that a man in anger is as wise as he that hath said over the four-and-twenty letters: or that a musket may be shot off as well upon the arm as upon a rest; and such other fond and high imaginations to think himself all in all. But, when all is done, the help of good counsel is that which setteth business straight; and if any man think that he will take counsel, but it shall be by pieces, asking counsel in one business of one man and in another business of another man, it is well—that is to say, better, perhaps, than if he asked none at all; but he runneth two dangers; one, that he shall not be faithfully counselled, for it is a rare thing, except it be from a perfect and entire friend, to have counsel given but such as shall be bowed and crooked to some ends which he hath that giveth it; the other, that he shall have counsel given hurtful and unsafe, though with good meaning, and mixed partly of mischief and partly of remedy; even as if you would call a physician that is thought good for the cure of the disease you complain of, but is unacquainted with your body, and therefore may put you in way for a present cure, but overthroweth your health in some other kind, and so cure the disease and kill the patient. But a friend that is wholly acquainted with a man's estate will beware, by furthering any present business, how he dasheth upon other inconvenience. And therefore rest not upon scattered counsels; they will rather distract and mislead than settle and direct.

After these two noble fruits of friendship (peace in the affections and support of the judgment) followeth the last fruit, which is like the pomegranate, full of many kernels. I mean aid, and bearing a part, in all actions and occasions. Here the best way to represent to life the manifold use of friendship is to cast and see how many things there are which a man cannot do himself; and then it will appear that it was a sparing speech of the ancients to say "that a friend is another himself," for that a friend is far more than himself. Men have their time, and die many times in desire of some things which they principally take to heart—the bestowing of a child, the finishing of a work, or the like. If a man have a true friend, he may rest almost secure that the care of those things will continue after him. So that a man hath, as it were, two lives in his desires. A man hath a body, and that body is confined to a place; but where friendship is, all offices of life are, as it were, granted to him and his deputy; for he may exercise them by his friend. How many things are there which a man cannot, with any face or comeliness, say or do himself? A man can scarce allege his own merits with modesty, much less extol them; a man cannot sometimes brook to supplicate or beg; and a number of the like. But all these things are graceful in a friend's mouth which are blushing in a man's own. So, again, a man's person hath many proper relations which he cannot put off. A man cannot speak to his son but as a father, to his wife but as a husband, to his enemy but upon terms; whereas a friend may speak as the case requires, and not as it sorteth with the person. But to enumerate these things were endless. I have given the rule; where a man cannot fitly play his own part, if he have not a friend, he may quit the stage.

FRIENDSHIP

RALPH WALDO EMERSON

"Take heed of thy friends. A faithful friend
is a strong defence, and he that hath found such
a one hath found a treasure."—*Proverbs*.

"Greater love hath no man than this; that a
man lay down his life for his friend."—*St. John*.

"Geteilte Freude, doppelte Freude;
Geteilter Schmerz, halber Schmerz."
—*German Proverb*.

FRIENDSHIP.

We have a great deal more kindness than is ever spoken. Maugre all the selfishness that chills like east winds the world, the whole human family is bathed with an element of love like a fine ether. How many persons we meet in houses, whom we scarcely speak to, whom yet we honor, and who honor us! How many we see in the street, or sit with in church, whom, though silently, we warmly rejoice to be with! Read the language of these wandering eye-beams. The heart knoweth.

The effect of the indulgence of this human affection is a certain cordial exhilaration. In poetry, and in common speech, the emotions of benevolence and complacency which are felt towards others, are likened to the material effects of fire; so swift, or much more swift, more active, more cheering are these fine inward irradiations. From the highest degree of passionate love, to the lowest degree of good will, they make the sweetness of life.

Our intellectual and active powers increase with our affection. The scholar sits down to write, and all his years of meditation do not furnish him with one good thought or happy expression; but it is necessary to write

a letter to a friend,—and, forthwith, troops of gentle
thoughts invest themselves, on every hand, with chosen
words. See in any house where virtue and self-respect
abide, the palpitation which the approach of a stranger
causes. A commended stranger is expected and an-
nounced, and an uneasiness betwixt pleasure and pain
invades all the hearts of a household. His arrival almost brings fear to the good hearts that would welcome
him. The house is dusted, all things fly into their
places, the old coat is exchanged for the new, and they
must get up a dinner if they can. Of a commended
stranger, only the good report is told by others, only
the good and new is heard by us. He stands to us for
humanity. He is, what we wish. Having imagined
and invested him, we ask how we should stand related
in conversation and action with such a man, and are uneasy with fear. The same idea exalts conversation with
him. We talk better than we are wont. We have the
nimblest fancy, a richer memory, and our dumb devil
has taken leave for the time. For long hours we can
continue a series of sincere, graceful, rich communications, drawn from the oldest, secretest experience, so
that they who sit by, of our own kinsfolk and acquaintance, shall feel a lively surprise at our unusual powers.
But as soon as the stranger begins to intrude his partialities, his definitions, his defects, into the conversation, it is all over. He has heard the first, the last and

best, he will ever hear from us.   He is no stranger now.
Vulgarity, ignorance, misapprehension, are old acquaint-
ances.   Now, when he comes, he may get the order, the
dress, and the dinner,—but the throbbing of the heart,
and the communications of the soul, no more.

Pleasant are these jets of affection which relume a
young world for me again.   Delicious is a just and firm
encounter of two, in a thought, in a feeling.   How
beautiful, on their approach to this beating heart; the
steps and forms of the gifted and the true!   The mo-
ment we indulge our affections, the earth is metamor-
phosed: there is no winter, and no night; all tragedies,
all ennuis vanish;—all duties even; nothing fills the pro-
ceeding eternity but the forms all radiant of beloved
persons.   Let the soul be assured that somewhere in the
universe it should rejoin its friend, and it would be content and cheerful alone for a thousand years.

I awoke this morning with devout thanksgiving for
my friends, the old and the new.   Shall I not call God,
the Beautiful, who daily showeth himself so to me in
his gifts?   I chide society, I embrace solitude, and yet
I am not so ungrateful as not to see the wise, the lovely,
and the noble-minded, as from time to time they pass
my gate.   Who hears me, who understands me, becomes mine—a possession for all time.   Nor is nature
so poor, but she gives me this joy several times, and
thus we weave social threads of our own, a new web of

relations; and, as many thoughts in succession substantiate themselves, we shall by-and-by stand in a new world of our own creation, and no longer strangers and pilgrims in a traditionary globe. My friends have come to me unsought. The great God gave them to me. By oldest right, by the divine affinity of virtue with itself, I find them, or rather, not I, but the Deity in me and in them, both deride and cancel the thick walls of individual character, relation, age, sex and circumstance, at which he usually connives, and now makes many one. High thanks I owe you, excellent lovers, who carry out the world for me to new and noble depths, and enlarge the meaning of all my thoughts. These are not stark and stiffened persons, but the new-born poetry of God —poetry without stop—hymn, ode, and epic, poetry still flowing, and not yet caked in dead books with annotation and grammar, but Apollo and the Muses chanting still. Will these, too, separate themselves from me again, or some of them? I know not, but I fear it not; for my relation to them is so pure that we hold by simple affinity, and the Genius of my life being thus social, the same affinity will exert its energy on whomsoever is as noble as these men and women, wherever I may be.

I confess to an extreme tenderness of nature on this point. It is almost dangerous to me to "crush the sweet poision of misused wine" of the affections. A

new person is to me always a great event, and hinders
me from sleep. I have had such fine fancies lately
about two or three persons as have given me delicious
hours; but the joy ends in the day: it yields no fruit.
Thought is not born of it; my action is very little mod-
ified. I must feel pride in my friend's accomplish-
ments as if they were mine—wild, delicate, throbbing
property in his virtues. I feel as warmly when he is
praised, as the lover when he hears applause of his en-
gaged maiden. We overestimate the conscience of our
friend. His goodness seems better than our goodness,
his nature finer, his temptations less. Everything that
is his, his name, his form, his dress, books, and instru-
ments, fancy enhances. Our own thought sounds new
and larger from his mouth.

Yet the systole and diastole of the heart are not without their analogy in the ebb and flow of love. Friendship, like the immortality of the soul, is too good to be
believed. The lover, beholding his maiden, half knows
that she is not verily that which he worships; and in the
golden hour of friendship we are surprised with shades
of suspicion and unbelief. We doubt that we bestow
on our hero the virtues in which he shines, and after-
wards worship the form to which we have ascribed this
divine inhabitation. In strictness, the soul does not respect men as it respects itself. In strict science, all
persons underlie the same condition of an infinite re-

moteness. Shall we fear to cool our love by facing the fact, by mining for the metaphysical foundation of this Elysian temple? Shall I not be as real as the things I see? If I am, I shall not fear to know them for what they are. Their essence is not less beautiful than their appearance, though it needs finer organs for its apprehension. The root of the plant is not unsightly to science, though for chaplets and festoons we cut the stem short. And I must hazard the production of the bald fact amidst these pleasing reveries, though it should prove an Egyptian skull at our banquet. A man who stands united with his thought, conceives magnificently of himself. He is conscious of a universal success, even though bought by uniform particular failures. No advantages, no powers, no gold or force can be any match for him. I cannot choose but rely on my own poverty, more than on your wealth. I cannot make your consciousness tantamount to mine. Only the star dazzles; the planet has a faint, moonlike ray. I hear what you say of the admirable parts and tried temper of the party you praise, but I see well that for all his purple cloaks I shall not like him, unless he is at last a poor Greek like me. I cannot deny it, O friend, that the vast shadow of the Phenomenal includes thee, also, in its pied and painted immensity,—thee, also, compared with whom all else is shadow. Thou art not Being, as Truth is, as Justice is,—thou art not my soul, but a

picture and effigy of that.   Thou hast come to me lately,
and already thou art seizing thy hat and cloak.   Is it
not that the soul puts forth friends, as the tree puts forth
leaves, and presently, by the germination of new buds,
extrudes the old leaf?   The law of nature is alternation
forevermore.   Each electrical state superinduces the op-
posite.   The soul environs itself with friends, that it
may enter into a grander self-acquaintance or solitude;
and it goes alone, for a season, that it may exalt its
conversation or society.   This method betrays itself
along the whole history of our personal relations.   Ever
the instinct of affection revives the hope of union with
our mates, and ever the returning sense of insulation
recalls us from the chase.   Thus every man passes his
life in the search after friendship, and if he should record his true sentiment, he might write a letter like this,
to each new candidate for his love.

DEAR FRIEND:—If I was sure of thee, sure of thy
capacity, sure to match my mood with thine, I should
never think again of trifles, in relation to thy comings
and goings.   I am not very wise: my moods are quite
attainable; and I respect thy genius: it is to me as yet
unfathomed; yet dare I not presume in thee a perfect
intelligence of me, and so thou art to me a delicious tor-
ment.   Thine ever, or never.

Yet these uneasy pleasures and fine pains are for
curiosity, and not for life.   They are not to be indulged.

This is to weave cobweb, and not cloth. Our friendships hurry to short and poor conclusions, because we have made them a texture of wine and dreams, instead of the tough fibre of the human heart. The laws of friendship are great, austere, and eternal, of one web with the laws of nature and of morals. But we have aimed at a swift and petty benefit, to suck a sudden sweetness. We snatch at the slowest fruit in the whole garden of God, which many summers and many winters must ripen. We seek our friend not sacredly, but with an adulterate passion which would appropriate him to ourselves. In vain. We are armed all over with subtle antagonisms, which, as soon as we meet, begin to play, and translate all poetry into stale prose. Almost all people descend to meet. All association must be a compromise, and, what is worst, the very flower and aroma of the flower of each of the beautiful natures disappears as they approach each other. What a perpetual disappointment is actual society, even of the virtuous and gifted! After interviews have been compassed with long foresight, we must be tormented presently by baffled blows, by sudden, unseasonable apathies, by epilepsies of wit and of animal spirits, in the hey-day of friendship and thought. Our faculties do not play us true, and both parties are relieved by solitude.

I ought to be equal to every relation. It makes no difference how many friends I have, and what content I

can find in conversing with each, if there be one to
whom I am not equal. If I have shrunk unequal from
one contest, instantly the joy I find in all the rest becomes mean and cowardly. I should hate myself, if
then I made my other friends my asylum.

> "The valiant warrior famoused for fight,
>   After a hundred victories, once foiled,
> Is from the book of honor razed quite,
>   And all the rest forgot for which he toiled."

Our impatience is thus sharply rebuked. Bashfulness
and apathy are a tough husk in which a delicate organi-
zation is protected from premature ripening. It would
be lost if it knew itself before any of the best souls were
yet ripe enough to know and own it. Respect the
naturlangsamkeit which hardens the ruby in a million
years, and works in duration, in which Alps and Andes
come and go as rainbows. The good spirit of our life
has no heaven which is the price of rashness. Love,
which is the essence of God, is not for levity, but for
the total worth of man. Let us not have this childish
luxury in our regards; but the austerest worth; let us
approach our friend with an audacious trust in the truth
of his heart, in the breadth, impossible to be overturned,
of his foundations.

The attractions of this subject are not to be resisted,
and I leave, for the time, all account of subordinate
social benefit, to speak of that select and sacred relation
which is a kind of absolute, and which even leaves the

language of love suspicious and common, so much is this purer, and nothing is so much divine.

I do not wish to treat friendships daintily, but with roughest courage. When they are real, they are not glass threads or frost-work, but the solidest thing we know. For now, after so many ages of experience, what do we know of nature, or of ourselves? Not one step has man taken toward the solution of the problem of his destiny. In one condemnation of folly stand the whole universe of men. But the sweet sincerity of joy and peace, which I draw from this alliance with my brother's soul, is the nut itself whereof all nature and all thought is but the husk and shell. Happy is the house that shelters a friend! It might well be built, like a festal bower or arch, to entertain him a single day. Happier, if he knew the solemnity of that relation, and honor its law! It is no idle band, no holiday engagement. He who offers himself a candidate for that covenant, comes up, like an Olympian, to the great games, where the first-born of the world are the competitors. He proposes himself for contests where Time, Want, Danger are in the lists, and he alone is victor who has truth enough in his constitution to preserve the delicacy of his beauty from the wear and tear of all these. The gifts of fortune may be present or absent, but all the hap in that contest depends on intrinsic nobleness, and the contempt of trifles. There are two elements that go to the composition of friendship, each so sovereign, that I can detect no superiority in either, no reason why either should be first named. One is Truth. A friend is a person with whom I may be sincere. Before him I may think aloud. I am arrived at last in the presence of a man so real and equal, that I may drop even those undermost garments of dissimulation, courtesy, and second thought, which men never put off, and may deal with him with the simplicity and wholeness with which one chemical atom meets another. Sincerity is the luxury allowed, like diadems and authority, only to the highest rank, *that* being permitted to speak truth, as having none above it to court or conform unto. Every man alone is sincere. At the entrance of a second person, hypocrisy begins. We parry and fend the approach of our fellow man by compliments, by gossip, by amusements, by affairs. We cover up our thought from him under a hundred folds. I knew a man who, under a certain religious frenzy, cast off this drapery, and omitting all compliment and commonplace, spoke to the conscience of every person he encountered, and that with great insight and beauty. At first he was resisted, and all men agreed he was mad. But persisting, as indeed he could not help doing, for some time in this course, he attained to the advantage of bringing every man of his acquaintance into true relations with him. No man would think of speaking falsely with him, or of putting him off with any chat of markets or reading rooms. But every man was constrained by so much sincerity to face him, and what love of nature, what poetry, what symbol of truth he had, he did certainly show him. But to most of us society shows not its face and eye, but its side and its back. To stand in true relations with men in a false age, is worth a fit of insanity, is it not? We can seldom go erect. Almost every man we meet requires some civility, requires to be humored;—he has some fame, some talent, some whim of religion or philanthropy in his head that is not to be questioned, and so spoils all conversation with him. But a friend is a sane man who exercises not my ingenuity but me. My friend gives me entertainment without requiring me to stoop, or to lisp, or to mask myself. A friend, therefore, is a sort of paradox in nature. I who alone am, I who see nothing in nature whose existence I can affirm with equal evidence to my own, behold now the semblance of my being in its height, variety and curiosity, reiterated in a foreign form; so that a friend may well be reckoned the masterpiece of nature.

The other element of friendship is Tenderness. We are holden to men by every sort of tie, by blood, by pride, by fear, by hope, by lucre, by lust, by hate, by admiration, by every circumstance and badge and trifle, but we can scarce believe that so much character can

subsist in another as to draw us by love. Can another
be so blessed, and we so pure, that we can offer
him tenderness? When a man becomes dear to me, I
have touched the goal of fortune. I find very little
written directly to the heart of this matter in books.
And yet I have one text which I cannot choose but remember. My author says, " I offer myself faintly and
bluntly to those whose I effectually am, and tender myself least to him to whom I am the most devoted." I
wish that friendship should have feet, as well as eyes
and eloquence. It must plant itself on the ground, before it walks over the moon. I wish it to be a little of
a citizen, before it is quite a cherub. We chide the
citizen because he makes love a commodity. It is an
exchange of gifts, of useful loans; it is good neighbor-
hood; it watches with the sick; it holds the pall at the
funeral; and quite loses sight of the delicacies and no-
bility of the relation. But though we cannot find the
god under this disguise of a sutler, yet, on the other
hand, we cannot forgive the poet if he spins his thread
too fine, and does not substantiate his romance by the
municipal virtues of justice, punctuality, fidelity and
pity. I hate the prostitution of the name of friendship
to signify modish and worldly alliances. I much prefer the company of plough-boys and tin-peddlers, to the
silken and perfumed amity which only celebrates its
days of encounter by a frivolous display, by rides in a

curricle, and dinners at the best taverns. The end of friendship is a commerce the most strict and homely that can be joined; more strict than any of which we have experience. It is for aid and comfort through all the relations and passages of life and death. It is fit for serene days, and graceful gifts, and country rambles, but also for rough roads and hard fare, shipwreck, poverty, and persecution. It keeps company with the sallies of the wit, and the trances of religion. We are to dignify to each other the daily needs and offices of man's life, and embellish it by courage, wisdom and unity. It should never fall into something usual and settled, but should be alert and inventive, and add rhyme and reason to what was drudgery.

For perfect friendship it may be said to require natures so rare and costly, so well tempered each, and so happily adapted, and withal so circumstanced (for even in that particular, a poet says, love demands that the parties be altogether paired), that very seldom can its satisfaction be realized. It cannot subsist in its perfection, say some of those who are learned in this warm lore of the heart, betwixt more than two. I am not quite so strict in my terms, perhaps because I have never known so high a fellowship as others. I please my imagination more with a circle of godlike men and women variously related to each other, and between whom subsists a lofty intelligence. But I find this law

of *one to one*, peremptory for conversation, which is the
practice and consummation of friendship. Do not mix
waters too much. The best mix as ill as good and bad.
You shall have very useful and cheering discourse at
several times with two several men, but let all three of
you come together, and you shall not have one new and
hearty word. Two may talk and one may hear, but
three cannot take part in a conversation of the most
sincere and searching sort. In good company there is
never such discourse between two, across the table, as
takes place when you leave them alone. In good company the individuals at once merge their egotism into a
a social soul exactly co-extensive with the several con-
sciousnesses there present. No partialities of friend to
friend, no fondnesses of brother to sister, of wife to husband, are there pertinent, but quite otherwise. Only
he may then speak who can sail on the common thought
of the party, and not poorly limited to his own. Now
this convention, which good sense demands, destroys
the high freedom of great conversation, which requires
an absolute running of two souls into one.

No two men but being left alone with each other enter into simpler relations. Yet it is affinity that deter-
mines *which* two shall converse. Unrelated men give
little joy to each other; will never suspect the latent
powers of each. We talk sometimes of a great talent
for conversation, as if it were a permanent property in

some individuals. Conversation is an evanescent relation—no more. A man is reputed to have thought and
eloquence; he cannot, for all that, say a word to his
cousin or his uncle. They accuse his silence with as
much reason as they would blame the insignificance of
a dial in the shade. In the sun it will mark the hour.
Among those who enjoy his thought he will regain his
tongue.

Friendship requires that rare mean betwixt likeness
and unlikeness, that piques each with the presence of
power and of consent in the other party. Let me be
alone to the end of the world, rather than that my
friend should overstep by a word or a look his real
sympathy. I am equally baulked by antagonism and
by compliance. Let him not cease an instant to be himself. The only joy I have in his being mine is that the
not mine is *mine.* It turns the stomach, it blots the
daylight, where I looked for a manly furtherance, or at
least a manly resistance, to find a mush of concession.
Better be a nettle in the side of your friend than his
echo. The condition which high friendship demands is
ability to do without it. To be capable of that high
office requires great and sublime parts. There must be
very two before there can be very one. Let it be an
alliance of two large formidable natures, mutually beheld, mutually feared, before yet they recognize the
deep identity which beneath these disparities unites them.

He only is fit for this society who is magnanimous: He must be so, to know its law. He must be one who is sure that greatness and goodness are always economy. He must be one who is not swift to intermeddle with his fortunes. Let him not dare to intermeddle with this. Leave to the diamond its ages to grow, nor expect to accelerate the births of the eternal. Friendship demands a religious treatment. We must not be wilful, we must not provide. We talk of choosing our friends, but friends are self-elected. Reverence is a great part of it. Treat your friend as a spectacle. Of course, if he be a man, he has merits that are not yours, and that you cannot honor, if you must needs hold him close to your person. Stand aside. Give those merits room. Let them mount and expand. Be not so much his friend that you can never know his peculiar energies, like fond mammas who shut up their boy in the house until he is almost grown a girl. Are you the friend of your friend's buttons, or of his thought? To a great heart he will still be a stranger in a thousand particulars, that he may come near in the holiest ground. Leave it to girls and boys to regard a friend as property, and to suck a short and all-confounding pleasure instead of the pure nectar of God.

Let us buy our entrance to this guild by a long probation. Why should we desecrate noble and beautiful souls by intruding on them? Why insist on rash per-

sonal relations with your friend? Why go to his
house or know his mother and brother and sisters?
Why be visited by him at your own? Are these things
material to our covenant? Leave this touching and
clawing. Let him be to me a spirit. A message, a
thought, a sincerity, a glance from him, I want, but
not news nor pottage. I can get politics, and chat, and
neighborly conveniences, from cheaper companions.
Should not the society of my friend be to me poetic,
pure, universal, and great as nature itself? Ought I to
feel that our tie is profane in comparison with yonder
bar of cloud that sleeps on the horizon, or that clump
of waving grass that divides the brook? Let us not
vilify, but raise it to that standard. That great defy-
ing eye, that scornful beauty of his mien and action, do
not pique yourself on reducing, but rather fortify and
enhance. Worship his superiorities. Wish him not
less by a thought, but hoard and tell them all. Guard
him as thy great counterpart; have a princedom to thy
friend. Let him be to thee forever a sort of beautiful
enemy, untamable, devoutly revered, and not a trivial
conveniency to be soon outgrown and cast aside. The
hues of the opal, the light of the diamond, are not to
be seen, if the eye is too near. To my friend I write a
letter, and from him I receive a letter. That seems to
you a little. Me it suffices. It is a spiritual gift
worthy of him to give and of me to receive. It pro-

fanes nobody. In these warm lines the heart will trust
itself, as it will not to the tongue, and pour out the
prophecy of a godlier existence than all the annals of
heroism have yet made good.

Respect so far the holy laws of this fellowship as not
to prejudice its perfect flower by your impatience for
its opening. We must be our own, before we can be
another's. There is at least this satisfaction in crime,
according to the Latin proverb; you can speak to your
accomplice on even terms. *Crimen quos inquinat æquat.*
To those whom we admire and love, at first we cannot.
Yet the least defect of self-possession vitiates, in my
judgment, the entire relation. There can never be deep
peace between two spirits, never mutual respect, until,
in their dialogue, each stands for the whole world.

What is so great as friendship, let us carry with what
grandeur of spirit we can. Let us be silent,—so we
may hear the whisper of the gods. Let us not inter-
fere. Who set you to cast about what you should say to
the select souls, or to say anything to such? No matter
how ingenious, no matter how graceful and bland.
There are innumerable degrees of folly and wisdom,
and for you to say aught is to be frivolous. Wait, and
thy soul shall speak. Wait until the necessary and
everlasting overpowers you, until day and night avail
themselves of your lips. The only money of God is
God. He pays never with any thing less or any thing

else. The only reward of virtue, is virtue; the only
way to have a friend, is to be one. Vain to hope to
come nearer a man by getting into his house. If
unlike, his soul only flees the faster from you, and
you shall catch never a true glance of his eye. We see
the noble afar off, and they repel us; why should we
intrude? Late—very late—we perceive that no arrange-
ments, no introductions, no consuetudes, or habits of
society would be of any avail to establish us in such relations with them as we desire,—but solely the uprise
of nature in us to the same degree it is in them: then
shall we meet as water with water: and if we should not
meet them then, we shall not want them, for we are already they. In the last analysis, love is only the reflection of a man's own worthiness from other men.
Men have sometimes exchanged names with their friends,
as if they would signify that in their friend each loved
his own soul.

The higher the style we demand of friendship, of
course the less easy to establish it with flesh and blood.
We walk alone in the world. Friends, such as we desire, are dreams and fables. But a sublime hope cheers
ever the faithful heart, that elsewhere in other regions
of the universal power, souls are now acting, enduring,
and daring, which can love us, and which we can love.
We may congratulate ourselves that the period of non-
age, of follies, of blunders, and of shame is passed in

solitude, and when we are finished men, we shall grasp heroic hands in heroic hands. Only be admonished by what you already see, not to strike leagues of friendship with cheap persons, where no friendship can be. Our impatience betrays us into rash and foolish alliances which no God attends. By persisting in your path, though you forfeit the little, you gain the great. You become pronounced. You demonstrate yourself, so as to put yourself out of the reach of false relations, and you draw to you the firstborn of the world,—those rare pilgrims whereof only one or two wander in nature at once, and before whom the vulgar great, show as spectres and shadows merely.

It is foolish to be afraid of making our ties too spiritual, as if we could lose any genuine love. Whatever correction of our popular views we make from insight, nature will be sure to bear us out in, and though it seem to rob us of some joy, will repay us with a greater. Let us feel, if we will, the absolute insulation of man. We are sure that we have all in us. We go to Europe, or we pursue persons, or we read books, in the instinctive faith that these will call it out and reveal us to ourselves. Beggars all. The persons are such as we; the Europe, an old faded garment of dead persons; the books, their ghosts. Let us drop this idolatry. Let us give over 'this mendicancy. Let us even bid our dearest friends farewell, and defy them, saying, "Who are you?

Unhand me: I will be dependent no more." Ah! seest
thou not, O brother, that thus we part only to meet
again on a higher platform, and only be more each
other's because we are more our own? A friend is
Janus-faced: he looks to the past and the future. He
is the child of all my foregoing hours, the prophet of
those to come. He is the harbinger of a greater friend.
It is the property of the divine to be reproductive.

I do then with my friends as I do with my books. I
would have them where I can find them, but I seldom
use them. We must have society on our own terms,
and admit or exclude it on the slightest cause. I can
not afford to speak much with my friend. If he is
great, he makes me so great that I cannot descend to
converse. In the great days, presentiments hover before me, far before me in the firmament. I ought then
to dedicate myself to them. I go in that I may seize
them. I go out that I may seize them. I fear only
that I may lose them receding into the sky, in which
now they are only a patch of brighter light. Then,
though I prize my friends, I cannot afford to talk with
them and study their visions, lest I lose my own.
It would indeed give me a certain household joy to
quit this lofty seeking, this spiritual astronomy, or
search of stars, and come down to warm sympathies
with you; but then I know well I shall mourn always
the vanishing of my mighty gods. It is true, next

week I shall have languid times, when I can well afford to occupy myself with foreign objects; then I shall regret the lost literature of your mind, and wish you were by my side again. But if you come, perhaps you will fill my mind only with new visions, not with yourself, but with your lustres, and I shall not be able any more than now to converse with you. So I will owe to my friends this evanescent intercourse. I will receive from them not what they have, but what they are. They shall give me that which properly they cannot give me, but which radiates from them. But they shall not hold me by any relations less subtle and pure. We will meet as though we met not, and part as though we parted not.

It has seemed to me lately more possible than I knew, to carry a friendship greatly, on one side, without due correspondence on the other. Why should I cumber myself with the poor fact that the receiver is not capacious? It never troubles the sun that some of his rays fall wide and vain into ungrateful space, and only a small part on the reflecting planet. Let your greatness educate the crude and cold companion. If he is unequal, he will presently pass away, but thou art enlarged by thy own shining; and, no longer a mate for frogs and worms, dost soar and burn with the gods of the empyrean. It is thought a disgrace to love unrequited. But the great will see that true love cannot be

unrequited. True love transcends instantly the unworthy
object, and dwells and broods on the eternal, and when
the poor, interposed mask crumbles, it is not sad, but
feels rid of so much earth, and feels its independency
the surer. Yet these things may hardly be said without a sort of treachery to the relation. The essence of
friendship is entireness, a total magnanimity and trust.
It must not surmise or provide for infirmity. It treats
its object as a god, that it may deify both.